Index

** INTRODUCTION **

Over the decades, Jávea has attracted everyone from fishermen, farmers to famous artists. Many newcomers arrive at Jávea and dive into its crystal waters and enjoy its vibrant beach life without any knowledge of its past. Jávea does not give up her secrets easily, especially if you don't speak the lingo!

As with all of my resource books, the goal is to teach you something about the historical backbone of a place in order to enhance your appreciation of its marvelous and magical manifestation.

If you have any questions, feel free to contact me.
Karla Ingleton Darocas
SpainLifestyle.com
KarlaDarocas.com

ROMAN ARCHES AND FISH FARMING IN ANCIENT XÀBIA

Karla Darocas Photography

Such was the level of luxury of the maritime enterprise of fish farming and salting that its owners added extra features like public hot spring bathing pools. Today, we can still see where the various ceramic tubes and other ceramic elements related to the heating systems of those structures were located.

The arched footbridges and other walkways are of outstanding construction with magnificent and unique views of the capes of San Martín and San Antonio as well as the mountain Montgó.

The Punta del Arenal in Xàbia is one of the largest remnants of a Roman fish farm in the Iberian peninsula, a site located at the northwest tip of the Bay of Xàbia and occupies a long stretch of tosca rock behind the Parador Hotel.

To the Romans, owning and controlling the sea was limited to the most powerful. The possession of VIVARIA PISCIUM (pools made by open channels on the coast to raise saltwater fish) became a symbol of social status.

It is called "Baños de la Reina" (Queens Baths), which is actually the name of all the fish breeding farms on the coast. There are others in Calpe and another in Campello. This surprising name is not Roman but was invented by the Islamic settlers.

The beach area known as Muntanyar was the name of a large Roman settlement that thrived for more than six hundred years, between the last decades of the 1st century BC to the 7th century. The population can only be estimated by the more than nine hundred burial pits that were discovered.

A series of elements combined to favour the presence of a Roman fish factory, dedicated to fishing and salting, at the Punta del Arenal.

First of all, the Greeks had previously defined this zone as a prime area for fishing tuna. Watchtowers, (hēmeroskópeion in Greek) were built along this coast to monitor and control the passage of schools of tuna in the annual migrations, hence this area served as the center of fishing operations.

Secondly, the existence of natural bays, where fish could be trapped, were close. The Bay of Jávea and Cala Blanca were the major trapping zones.

Thirdly, freshwater for cleaning the fish was available from the channel of La Fontana where there was a natural spring and the river Gorgos which could be dammed to create a reservoir.

Lastly, a natural salt marsh, a place where salt water is trapped and allowed to evaporate leaving only the salt, was not too far away in the area called "El Saladar". The Punta de Castell is where the "Séquia de la Nòria", a large channel cut and excavated into the tosca, is located. This channel was used to allow the seawater to come into the salt marsh.

Within the fish-farm complex are found deposits for fish preparation, a large nursery tank, and other tanks of different sizes. Some are made from mortar and lime masonry supported on rammed earth. Others are carved directly into the tosca stone and coated with lime mortar and crushed red clay ceramic. Some are carved rock with no inner lining. Most have a circular hole carved into the rock beside a square hole, no doubt to fit their dolliums, large ceramic pots with stone caps used for storage.

It has been reported on many websites that the Punta del Arenal fish farm was also in the business of making "garum"(a stinky fish sauce made from fish guts), but according to Gabriela Martin, a well-researched author on the subject, this was not the case.

In her research paper, The Roman Fisheries Of The Coast Of Alicante, she notes that on her evaluation of the Punta del Arenal, she did not find any remains of "garum bottles nor garum amphorae". Hence in her speculation, from studies on other sites that indeed made "garum" that this fish farm was dedicated to tuna and the industry was packing the tuna in brine to be shipped in amphorae.

She also points out that on the Alicante coast there is still a large amount of salted dried tuna consumed. It is found everywhere in Alicante and Valencia under the name of "tonyina de sorra".

Research notations...

* Gabriela Martin; The Roman Fisheries Of The Coast Of Alicante

* Gabriela Martin and Maria Dolores Serres; The Roman fishing factory of Idvea (Alicante). Various Works Series of Prehistoric Research Service. Provincial Council of Valencia (in press).

* Gabriela Martin; The supposed Greek colony of Hemeroskopeion. Archaeological study of the Denia-Ivea area. Papers of the Archeology Laboratory of Valencia, NA Faculty of Philosophy and Letters of Valencia 1968.

XÀBIA , JOSÉ ANTONIO BOLUFER AND HIS SHIP MYSTERY

This is a story about a small village, a large wharf, a visionary businessman, his sailing fleet, and a tiny treat of dried fruit.

Pailebot PEPE TONO. From the book Xabia Marinera. Graphic Memory

The Xàbia wharf was finished in 1879 and all of the small fishing boats and transport barges that would normally be stranded on the beach could now properly anchor. The large size of the wharf allowed for the berthing of a variety of boats, many of them owned by the main merchants of Xàbia.

On any given day, the ships that moored in Xàbia were Feluccas, a traditional Mediterranean wooden sailing boat; Jabeques, a triangular sailboat, with which one could also sail by rowing; Schooners, a type of sailing vessel with fore-and-aft sails on two or more masts; and Pailebotes, a type of sailing vessel that has had various uses: merchant, fishing or recreational yacht.

The ability to load and unload directly from land with greater speed and security increased port traffic with not only the export of raisins, almonds, peanuts, onions, dried figs, wine, etc.- but also imports from England and America like guano, coal, cast iron for balconies and "mobila" wood.

The diets of the Xábia citizens changed with the new imports like sugar, coffee, chocolate, chicory, tobacco, carbonates, and salts. There were also new styles of earthenware and fabrics to enrich the homes of Xàbia.

These numerous supplies needed to be stored and warehouses sprang up and sawmills and even a toy factory.

The economic boom of the agricultural trade encouraged the managers of the wharf to request an expansion of the port to provide greater efficiency. The growth of the port traffic, moving goods and people forced the public administration to establish a customs service, a health department, a maritime department, and a telegraph cable service between the Peninsula and the Balearic Islands.

Reconstruction of the Bolufer warehouse in the gardens of the Sultana. From the book Xàbia Marinera. Graphic Memory

The pastoral raisin trade became a yearly concern that occupied an abundant workforce during the final months of summer and the first months of autumn. The process began in mid-August with the harvesting, blanching, and drying of the grapes.

Once the grapes were converted into raisins the farmers became merchants.

The storage warehouses by the sea became busy with an army of women and children separating the different qualities and plucking the stems and packing the boxes that were covered with local trade labels destined to foreign markets.

The traders of Xábia were able to infiltrate the British market with their large and seedy muscatel raisins and evict the Cyprus, Crete, and Turkey exports of "Corinth" seedless raisins or currents that were small.

The popularity of the Xàbia raisin flourished because of its size and nutritional value that was utilized by Anglo-Saxon workers, whether deep in minds or out on the high seas. In the high society circles of the British empire, the raisins of Xàbia were a necessary ingredient of their famous "Christmas pudding".

Still today, the Xàbia trademark name "Sultana" that was clearly displayed on boxes of raisins shipped by the House of Bolufer acts as a beacon to the success of the town and its wharf. Bolufer named his shipping warehouse Sultana too, as he appreciated the power of the Sultan and wanted his empire to be powerful too.

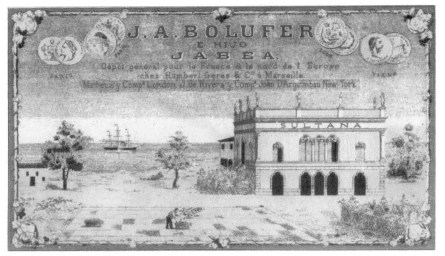

Box Label on raisins of Casa Bolufer Warehouse From the book Xàbia Marinera. Graphic Memory

JOSÉ ANTONIO BOLUFER

Xàbia-based shipowner José Antonio Bolufer Cruañes (1814-1890) made a lot of money being a merchant of raisins and other commodities, with a large warehouse in Duanes de la Mar in the Port of Xábia. He also built a mansion in the Church Square in Xábia that still attracts attention today.

A graduate of the University of Valencia where he received his doctorate in law, he went on to build an impressive shipping company featuring some of the most famous ships on the Mediterranean.

The fleet included PEPE TONO (Capt. Bartolomé Morato), SULTANA (Capt. Valentin Ros), MARIA (Capt. Francisco Ros) and LEON (Capt. Bartolomé Mengual).

In 1855, he received the title of Knight Commander of the Royal Order of Isabella the Catholic.

HIS PRIDE AND JOY

PEPE TONO was a pailebot or pilot's boat and the best and most important of the ships in his fleet, which was born as a consequence of the economic bubble that came about due to the demand for raisins.

According to the newspaper El Constitucional, in the December 15th edition, 1877, it was noted in a letter to the editor that the townsfolk of Xábia witnessed the launch of the Pepe Tono.

The author of the letter marked the importance of the ship to the town as it was built on the seashore by the rich merchant D. José Antonio Bolufer.

About the launch, he says, "It is astonishing the simplicity with which the sailors and caulkers of our coast carry out the operation, always risky, of beaching a ship, with no other assistance than some pieces of wood, four very bad cables, and two rickety winches. Truth is that the state of the sea, almost always quiet in this safe bay, made the operation much easier; but it is also true that it was a surprising sight to see more than a thousand people in whose faces were painted fear and hope during the critical moment when the ship glided gently on the inclined plane of wood on which her keel rested until she saw free of its moorings floating in a calm and fanciable sea."

On February 11, 1890, José Antonio Bolufer died.

The last news of the Pepe Tono was found in the Madrid Heraldo newspaper on Sunday, October 22, 1893. It announced that Pepe Tono set sail from Malaga heading to Havana on the 21 of that month.

What happened to the ship from that moment -- no one knows.

Many ships that made that trek were sold when they arrived in Havana, but specifically, about the Pepe Tono, no one knows what happened? Was it lost at sea? Was it sold and the name was changed?

To this day, it is a mystery.

SOROLLA FINDS INSPIRATION IN XÀBIA
FOR A SPECIAL PATRON

When Joaquín Sorolla first came to Xàbia in 1896, it was to witness grape farmers in harvest as well as the marvelous raisin industry that had taken hold of Europe with its rich flavoured and nutritional snack.

He had received a commission to create two unique vertical panel paintings to flank a door, of which the particular dimensions were to match. The theme was to celebrate the wine industry. Their composition and style were to be neoclassical, as this was the artistic genre of the early twentieth century, preferred by the bourgeoisie circles.

The patron was a wealthy Chilean, Rafael Errázuriz Urmeneta who was a politician, diplomat, businessman, and grape farmer.

The patron became fascinated with Sorolla and his work while on a European trip which landed him in Madrid. He ended up commissioning Sorolla to create a variety of works from 1896 to 1905 including a family portrait.

However, in the summer of 96 Sorolla had spent his vacation at his summer residence on the beach of Cabanyal, an eccentric fishing area of Valencia, where he created many of his masterpieces.

Sorolla was only 33 years old and already had a wife, Clotilde, and three children María, Joaquín, and Elena. He left them in October to travel down the coast and witness the grape harvest in Dénia and Xàbia.

His plan was to research the subject for a panel painting called the Grape Press.

The composition is presented in a classical way with much of the canvas taken up with the main characters. A man is clad in a Roman or Greek-style toga draped over his hardy body. He is using his weight to press the grapes while the child is collecting the juice. The tree that supports the press is probably a carob or olive tree.

The painting clearly demonstrates the season as the grape leaves have their autumn gold colour. They are not detailed and we must speculate that they are indeed grapes.

What captures the attention of anyone who knows Xàbia is the beautiful Mediterranean blue sky on a clear day that highlights the iconic Cape San Martin (Cap Martí)

According to documentation, Sorolla did his sketches of the area and made notes, and then returned to his studio in Madrid to create this work using a variety of historical books to draft the press.

In another panel called The Grape Harvest (La Vendemia), which was crafted in 1896, again to suit the demand of his patron, we find a stylized woman in Greek robes caught in the act of picking grapes. Again, the landscape is Xàbia but the grapes are not the green Muscatel variety but instead a dark purple grape suggesting the Chilean types.

10 years later, Rafael Errázuriz Urmeneta traveled to Madrid with his family and commissioned Sorolla to paint a family portrait which he paid an astronomical price of forty thousand pesetas (approx 240 thousand euros).

You would think that at such a price, the painting was a grand work but Sorolla completed it in only 12 days.

The composition of this family portrait combines the sophistication of Velazquez, almost a tribute to Las Meninas, with the opulence of a bourgeoisie individuality.

Errázuriz's Chilean wife maintains the central focal point and axis of the painting. She is surrounded by her flock of five girls and a boy. She transmits a subtle elegance.

The whole group, except for the father, looks at Sorolla.

THE TALE OF SOROLLA'S HOLIDAY HORROR IN JÁVEA

It was the summer of 1905 when the talented Valencian impressionist painter Joaquín Sorolla brought his family to the Port of Jávea (Playa de la Grava) for a much-needed holiday.

Clotilde and Elena in the rocks of Jávea (1905. Private collection)

Inspired by the cliffs of both the Cape of San Antonio and La Nao, and the turquoise sparkle of the east-facing sea, Sorolla explored some of his greatest impressionist experiments by capturing the light and underwater movements.

A dedicated artist, Sorolla spent his holiday at work. However, to allow his family the freedom to swim, sun, and enjoy their time on holiday too, Sorolla hired a nanny/maid to watch their youngest child Elena, cook, tidy, and do their laundry at their 11 cents per day rental accommodation.

Unknown to the Sorolla family, this maid had a very jealous military boyfriend from Murcia who was going to turn their happy holiday into a hellish horror!

Versions of this story have circulated around Jávea since 1905.

It wasn't until April 2016 when the Denia-based journalist and historian Antoni Reig began to shed light on the truth on this terrible tale by publishing a book about historical crimes collected from old newspapers. His findings were published in his award-winning collection of essays, Històries de Crims i Criminals of the Marina Alta (Crime and Criminal Stories of the Marina Alta).

He managed to find a criminal report dated August 26th, 1905 about the event which took place in the Aduanas del Mar region of the Grava beach where there were several large homes built by wealthy local families.

The report states that the events developed between six or seven in the morning and that it turned into a "bloody and vulgar drama" that filled the neighbourhood with "dismay" because they were unaccustomed to witnessing such horrible events.

Aduanas del Mar and La Grava beach, Xàbia around 1920.

THE EVENT

August 21st is the day to which this account has its origin. The reporter spins the tale by stating that it involved a servant girl by the name of Ramona Sánchez, from Madrid, aged 23, who had been working for the Sorolla family for a year.

The girl had established a relationship with a civil guard in Murcia by the name of Bartolomé Güeras, who was widowed and had three children.

According to the reporter about their relationship, he states that the "relations had in a short time reached a degree of dangerous intimacy" probably because it had fostered a passion that Ramona did not return.

The reporter continues to explain that during the Sorolla family's stays in Jávea, Ramona had received letters from her suitor but never bothered to answer them. The boyfriend took it upon himself to travel to Jávea and confront Ramona and demand an explanation.

Bartolomé searched for her and finally found Ramona with another maid named Asunción at the community laundry. He stayed with the two girls while they did their washing and when finished, he escorted them to the door of the holiday residence of the Sorolla family.

According to Asunción, who I suspect was an interviewed witness, Bartolomé talked with Ramona in a "low voice" and she would answer him "coldly".

It was at the door of the residence that Bartolomé grabbed Ramona's arm and held on tight as she fought to escape his clutch. He reached for a gun. There is no reference as to what type of gun, but since he was described as a "Carabinero", which is a member of the civil guard who carries a bolt-action rifle, I can only assume that this was the type of gun he grabbed?

The distressed boyfriend shot Ramona in the back and then in one quick move, aimed the gun at his head and pulled the trigger.

I found another brief newspaper report in the ABC newspaper dated the 24th of August, 1905.

It says, "In the house where the painter Sorolla lives in Jávea, Bartolomé Güeras fired a shot at the servant Ramona Sánchez, with whom he held a romantic relationship. The girl was seriously injured. The aggressor committed suicide."

A B C. JUEVES 24 DE AGOSTO DE 1905. PAG. 12

Crimen y suicidio.
    Valencia, 23, 12 n. En la casa de campo que en Jávea habita el pintor Sorolla, ha disparado un tiro Bartolomé Guerás á la sirviente Ramona Sánchez, con quien sostenía relaciones amorosas.
    La muchacha resultó gravemente herida. El agresor se suicidó.—*Muñoz*.

ACCORDING TO SOROLLA

The family was freaked out, to say the least. They managed to put the incident behind them and continue their holiday and Sorolla his work, but Sorolla did write to his friend Pedro Gil on August 30th, 1905 with some details of this frightful event.

In the letter, Sorolla explains to his friend that he was sorry for not writing for a while but that over the past week or so, he had been so sick that he could "barely move".

He says, "It took me a long time to write to you because unfortunately I had to suffer about three days in bed, due to my discomfort, but thank God everything went well, but when I was going to get out of bed, a bloody drama occurred whose sad event upset me and Clotilde, who was quite affected. It would be 7 in the morning, while we were all still in bed, we heard three shots, shouts, running, and, since I could not get out of bed, Clotilde did and managed to witness a horrible scene. Our cook had a boyfriend in Madrid, he was a civil guard and he showed up in Jávea and he tried to kill her, wounding her alone and killing himself later."

So, here the accounts by Sorolla are pretty much the same as the newspaper report, except that Sorolla thinks that the boyfriend was from Madrid, not Murcia as reported.

Swimmers of Jávea (1905. Sorolla Museum)

TRUTH TO THE HEARSAY

The story of this cruel act of passion and suicide begs the question: Why?

The gossip around Jávea for many years was that the maid must have been in a love affair with the famous, yet aging, Sorolla. Was this imagined love triangle the reason that the daring civil guard had produced a jealous mind?

To anyone of the era who had read the report in the Alicante newspaper might have drawn the same conclusion as it was reported that Ramona, the maid, was a beauty. He reports that "She is a woman of regular height, dark, big eyes, and a sweet look".

Of course, Sorolla's family denied the gossip.

Further research concluded that there were no hard clues to this illicit romantic affair in any of Sorolla's letters or even in his account to the reporter.

In a letter to his good friend Gil Moreno, for whom he shared a deep intimate personal relationship, it is impossible to suspect that he hid any secrets from him. Gil Moreno's friendship with Sorolla was such a trusting one, that often Sorolla would ask Moreno to sign paintings that he had forgotten.

In the testimony to the reporter, Sorolla talks about the tragedy without any noticeable emotion, even though the event occurred on his doorstep. He does not suffer any intimate pain about the circumstances and waves it off as an illogical act of humanity. He does not even know the maid Ramona's name and only refers to her as "the cook" and he certainly never highlights her beauty.

Again, the rumours and local gossip remarks how Sorolla was so upset by the death of the maid, that he never returned to Jávea ever again. This is also not the truth!

In January 1919, he returned to Jávea and wrote his wife a letter whereby he recounts actually visiting the holiday rental.

He says, "Imagine my surprise to find myself in the place where good and bad times we spent. It left me sad as we went through the crime house and remembered the scare."

He doesn't lament on the house of horror but instead remembers the good times.

He says, "We went through the place where I painted such beautiful things with you and my beloved Elena. What color. What beauty! The sea was calm and all the yellows and oranges were reflected and it seemed that we traveled on a sea of gold to red ."

The bath, Javea, 1905 - Joaquín Sorolla

JÁVEA - ONE HUNDRED MILES SOUTH OF VALENCIA

Aureliano de Beruete painted by Sorolla

This is a translated portion of a travel account written by Aureliano de Beruete (eminent historian and critic of art) when he visited the Valencian impressionist / historical painter Joaquín Sorolla, who was on holiday in Jávea 1905.

Original in Spanish Copyright, 1909, by THE HISPANIC SOCIETY OF AMERICA

One hundred miles south of Valencia, a little-used narrow-gauge railway brings us through an opulent country to a shack of a railway station known as Vergel. The only train that brings you there in the day arrives exactly at noon. From the station, there is nothing to see save a miserable country restaurant across the way and a blazing white road that stretches away in radiant sunlight across the treeless plain.

That twelve-mile ride in the tumble-down Vergel diligence is not a tempting prospect, but it is the opening of the door of Jávea, a hidden Paradise where Sorolla has done a great part of his outdoor work.

Those twelve miles are very, very long. The dust powders you as white as it has silvered the vineyard by the wayside. The fat lady who had come with her maid to spend two weeks in the country with her family, cries, "Dios, que calor," and swears by all the saints that the climate is changing and that the summers are surely warmer than when she was a girl. Her servant pulls close the curtains of the crazy vehicle to keep out the light and the dust.

We lumber through many a Spanish village with its white-washed walls, gay doors, and windows, dominating church, staring faces. What strikes one as very curious is to find electric lights in most of these villages that are absolute without other evidence of modern civilization. Ahead of one in the plain looms Montgo, a mountain of naked rock. For it, the road makes a vast detour, and at the crest of a little hill, we look at last upon Jávea.

An Arab town is your first thought. In a confused mass of white-walled houses, half-revealed rose gardens, and beaten, unpaved roads, the town creeps down to its beach.

The violet of the bay is held at the sides by the splendor of two great capes, San Antonio and Nao. Their walls of rock sweep far out into the sea and form the most eastern projection of Spain in the Mediterranean.

Blocked from north and south by these sentinels, backed by Montgo, the town sleeps as though lulled by its hushing sea, by the sighing cypresses about its well-trodden Calvary. The town has no hotel; Baedeker * is unknown. A slattern woman, at one wretched place, after prodigious scurrying about by her husband to buy provisions, serves you two fried eggs, a piece of cold fish, and some black olives.

A walk through the town will take you past some of the great raisin warehouses. Inside, in the semi- gloom, hundreds of women are stemming raisins for shipment to England. As they work, they sing in honor of the Virgin, a dragging canticle that echoes through the ancient arches of the place and out into the still afternoon air.

Life is in every way most primitive and living is very cheap. A furnished house near the quay may be rented for eleven cents a day, but beware, unless you bring an establishment of servants with you from Madrid, you may find little to eat. There is no ice and little meat.

Butter is a messy mass brought in a tin from Switzerland or even Denmark, and it is served day after day in the same tin until it becomes a rancid offense. Inquiry elicits a fabled report that a certain very rich man actually has some cows on a farm far away, but that their milk is precious beyond selling, and is sent only as a gift of great price to those far gone in sickness. Goats' milk only maybe had. Antonio drives the goats to your place and milks them just before your breakfast, and the milk is drunk warm before it spoils with the heat. "My milk is better than Vicente's," says the goat herder. "I know the best places in the mountain where there is grass." This he says with the air of a botanist announcing the secret of a bed of rarest orchids. Meat is covered thick with salt and hung in a tin pail down a well.

A hapless artist who would prefer to live near the sea, must throw himself on the mercy of Paquita, who may or may not be willing to cook for him in the backroom of her grocery. Without butter, everything is fried or boiled with olive oil. The cooking is done out of doors over a tiny fire of twigs.

The fish is delightful, so are the melons, but strange, crawly things of the sea are served as you have only seen before in alcohol bottles in zoological museums. Occasionally, on opening a soup tureen, you find floating on the surface of the oil soup a good-sized fish, boiled, head and all. Its single visible eye stares at you glassily, and you replace the cover of the dish and turn to find what further adventure dinner may bring you.

Jávea is the ideal place for a painter. There are no newspapers, no letters, no engagements. One paints from dawn to dusk. It is the huge, tawny rocks of the place under the pitiless and searching illumination of the sun of Alicante that supplies the characteristic printable note of the place.

Here Sorolla has shown us wonderful studies of the children of the port at play, as in the remarkable study of the boy hunting mussels. These happy little savages play about all day in a freedom undisturbed by problems of primary education. "Is there a river between New York and England?" asked a sixteen-year-old girl, at Jávea, "or is London separated from England only by mountains?"

It was in the limpid waters of this port that Sorolla undertook the solution of a problem of the swirl of sun-pierced water about a human figure. Of this subject, he made several preliminary studies, and then in four afternoons of brisk work produced his large canvas. The composition for this picture was scrawled on the side of his house in charcoal while servants were busy stretching the big canvas for the work. The picture was painted, of course, directly from nature, the stretcher being tied with ropes to some posts which had been arranged temporarily on a ledge of rock first chiseled smooth for the purpose. Six urchins served in relays as models, three swimming round and round for the painter, while three rested and warmed themselves in the sun.

Of his own family bathing among the rocks of Jávea, he has shown us some delightful pictures that reflect all the gaiety, radiant happiness, and intimacy of the scene. Plunging about in the swinging sea and clear waters of these secret glens, with the laughter of the Sorolla children echoing back from the rocks about, it seems impossible to believe that there is anything in the world but youth and laughter and success.

The colors at Jávea are almost unbelievable. Above, a cloudless sky of violet-blue is broken by the mounting yellow walls of Cabo San Antonio, all about the rock formations are brilliant with embedded stones of every hue, while every swirl of the water discovers a wealth of color in the swinging, growing plants that find their home in the sea.

"I can't paint that," "I can't paint that," Sorolla often says of these incidents at Jávea. "Everybody would only say it was made up in the studio." And then he adds, "As far as outdoor work is concerned, a studio is only a garage; a place in which to store pictures and repair them, never a place in which to paint them."

(* Karl Baedeker on July 1, 1827, was a German publisher and pioneer in the business of worldwide travel guides.)

WHO WAS ANDRÉ LAMBERT WITHIN THE HISTORY OF JÁVEA ARTS?

Ermita de Santa LLucia

André Lambert Jordán (1884-1967) was a watercolorist, painter, engraver, and Swiss-French architect who lived a large part of his life in Javea. For Lambert, Jávea was a gold mine of interest and he made many artworks about the place from historical buildings to the unique landscape.

André Lambert was born in Switzerland on March 17, 1884, where he studied architecture at the School of Advanced Technical Studies in Munich. Later he went on to study Fine Arts in the Bavarian capital and it was these studies that ended him in Paris around 1908.

André established his first studio in Montparnasse, later moving to the Ile St. Louis.

In the French capital, he surrounded himself with a select group of intellectuals, poets, and artists.

Inclined towards graphic work, he began to illustrate books around 1912. He also collaborated with the magazine Simplicissimus, a weekly satirical magazine written in German founded by Albert Langen in April 1896 and published until 1967.

In 1919 Paris, he founded the Latin magazine Janus in collaboration with Georges Aubault and was a contributor to the magazine Vita Latina, published in Avignon.

In 1912, he traveled to Spain for the first time, discovering and studying the gypsy types and customs.

After marrying his wife, Raquel, he settled in "Cala Blanca" area of Jávea, where his house still stands to this day. André repopulated his land and surrounding area with white pines and rebuilt a ruin into a villa that followed the architectural typology of the region. Neighbours started to call the area the "Cala del Francés", due to this reformation.

Lambert made many watercolors and engravings of the urban center and rural environment around Jávea. The artist always felt very linked to Jávea, both artistically and emotionally.

André Lambert died in Paris on November 24, 1967, his remains being cremated and moved to Jávea, where they were buried under the pines, in the "Cala Blanca".

The paintings and engravings of Lambert are characterized by their refined modernist style, where certain symbolist influences have a great inclination, especially in the line of Greco-Roman classicism, which was popular with the bourgeoisie of the time period.

Today, citizens and visitors will find a preserved palace in the heart of Jávea that shows the Lambert name. This is Casa Lambert, a community visual arts school and artist exhibition sponsored by the family of the French-Swiss painter, André Lambert.

Fig. 1

XÀBIA / JÁVEA REGIONAL HERITAGE REWARDS RAISINS

The Marina Alta region, especially the coastal village of Jávea/Xàbia, has its 20th-century heritage wrapped up in raisins. Not just any raisins, but the succulent Sultana raisins made from the marvelous muscatel grapes, which brought fame and wealth to these industrious villagers.

Xàbia artist, teacher, and resident Soler Blasco (1920-1984) became an important local figure because he was the mayor from 1974 to 1979. He was also involved in great cultural projects such as the creation of an archaeological museum and the Municipal Public Library.

Within the Soler Blasco Archaeological and Ethnographic Museum are an important series of artworks by Soler Blasco that immortalize traditional trades, fiestas, and legends. One of these impressionistic paintings showcases the process of blanching and drying of grapes to make raisins.

Blanching accelerated the drying process. It all started with lighting the oven or fire, "el fogater", then filling a pot with water, herbs, caustic soda, and bringing it to a boil. Then the grapes were tossed into the pot for a good 15-minute boil, then spooned out onto a drying mat.

In the back of this painting by Soler Blasco you can see the landmark mountain named "Montgo" and a white building with a "Riurau". During the 19th and 20th centuries, Riuraus flooded the entire Marina Alta rural landscape. These unique Roman arched constructions were used to dry the raisins when it rained.

BRIEF HISTORY

The technique of blanching grapes goes back two millennia. In the writings of Julius Moderatus Columella, a prominent scholar on agriculture in the Roman empire, he describes 'l'escaldà' ". This information comes from Josep Antoni Gisbert, the archaeologist, and director of Denia's Ethnological Museum.

The oldest documented sources relating to the production of raisins in the Valencian territory date back to the second half of the 15th century. In the Marina Alta, there is evidence of the production dated 1476, whereby Valencian merchants wrote out billing contracts with Morisco farmers who lived in Dénia, Xàbia, Xaló, Pedreguer, and Ondara, for their supply of raisins.

After the expulsion of the Moors and Moriscos in 1609, the grape production disappeared and so did the raisins because the Christians did not know the procedure.

It was actually because of travelers to the Marina Alta and La Safor regions in the 1800s who prompted the production of raisins again, especially the English Navy who wanted raisins to combat scurvy and other diseases because of poor diet, but also the miners and textile factory workers wanted raisins to keep in their pockets to fight fatigue.

HERITAGE FESTIVAL

Each year, the celebration of the "Escaldá de la Pasa" takes place in the village of Jesus Pobre on the last morning of August. The villagers keep their heritage alive by recreating the process of making raisins via blanching. The ritual lasts all morning and ends with traditional dances.

Below is a small impressionist work by Joaquín Sorolla on his visit in 1900. It is called *Scalding grapes, Jávea*. He has captured an image of a boy taking great care with the fire used to boil the water. In the background are several figures actually doing the scalding and then preparing them for drying. On the left, two men dropping off boxes, and in front of them, are several esparto grass baskets. The scene takes place inside a riurau.

THE JÁVEA MONUMENT THAT NO ONE TALKS ABOUT!

There is a monument in Jávea, right around the corner to the main square, that is a remarkable piece of historical and architectural value, but no one in Jávea ever talks about it.

Karla Darocas Photography

When I discovered it, I was quick to admire its Valencian Gothic architecture with a proud ribbed vault with an exterior of Isabelline style decorations, popular with the Crown of Castile during the reign of Catholic Monarchs.

This fabulous monument standing in front of me was made from sandstone blocks or tosca, as was the traditional building material chiseled from the seashore of this village as a cheap and easy building substance.

I noticed a shield with a raised iconic graphic of an oxen yoke and arrows, which was the logo or symbol for the Spanish co-monarchy of the Catholic Monarchs, namely Ferdinand II of Aragon and Isabella I of Castile. It served as a visual statement or tribute to these Catholic rulers. It was their marriage that managed to united Spain and bring fame and heroic virtues to their families. It was also a graphic glorification to the names of the monarchs: Y stood for "yugo" (span. yoke) and for "Ysabel" (in ancient spelling) and F stood for "flechas" (span. arrows) and for Fernando.

Other Isabelline motifs that presented themselves on the exterior of this structure were the round "beads" or "orbs" that thread their way around the monument. It also celebrated the upward and elegant "ogee arches" that are built into the facade. These pretty arches may look arabesque and Muslim but they are very much Gothic and Catholic of the Isabelline period.

On the other side, once again the Isabelline motifs prevail include the corner pinnacles rising up to the sky and the fantastic animal gargoyles, which separate heaven and earth from evil and act as imaginative water spouts so that rain won't dribble down and damage the monument.

This is all the information that I took in, at my first glance at this perfectly square structure.

However, on my second inspection, I realized that the heraldic shields were different. The pronounced crest on the upper point of one of the Gothic arches was the same as Catholic Monarchs but not the same.

This heraldic shield was divided into four with the coats of arms of Castile, León, Aragon, and Navarre, plus the enté-en-point or apex for Granada. There were also the arrows and the yoke, again representing the Catholic Monarchs. Plus, popping out the top of the shield was a proud eagle representing the Eagle of Saint John the Evangelist, which Queen Isabella

I of Castile used on her evangelist crest. However, this eagle looked more masculine than the ones I have seen in my travels.

It seemed that the whole purpose of this architectural structure was to protect a giant Apostle's Cross, again made from tosca stone.

Franco shield

I took some photos of the monument and went home to do my research and put a name and story to my discovery!

However, it was with grave frustration that I could not find anything on TripAdvisor or any of the official tourist type websites about this gem of architecture?

So, I contacted some friends who are Jáveaites, born and bred, and they knew nothing about it?

I had another friend contact a local historian, and all he said was that this monument was not "talked about". I didn't know what that was supposed to mean?

I finally found this newspaper article, from 2015, that cleared up the mystery.

http://lamarinaplaza.com/2015/08/28/xabia-aprueba-el-proyecto-que-eliminara-sus-simbolos-franquistas/

THE MYSTERY UNVEILS...

The name of the monument is called "la Cruz Cubierta de la Plaza del Trinquet" and it was built, not in the era of the Catholic Monarchs of the 1400s, like the famous church of San Bartolomé, which stands just around the corner. No, this monument was in fact built in 1954.

Franco shield, not Catholic Monarchs

Yes, indeed it mimics the 15th-century Valencian Gothic vaulting techniques and Isabelline designs but it was built by Francoists as a tribute to their "fallen" soldiers. The shields that flanked the facades were not tributes to the Catholic Monarchs but adopted symbols to enhance Franco's coat of arms. He had taken the existing Spanish crown identifiers and modified them to suit his new state of government.

According to this article in the La Marina Plaza online newspaper, Jávea had been asked to destroy the monument with respect to a law that prohibited Franco symbols in public places. The law is called "Ley de Memoria Histórica" and it was approved by the Congress of Deputies on 31 October 2007.

The law is quite intensive and you can read all about it on Wikipedia, but in a nutshell, and what concerns us here, is the following:

"The law establishes that "shields, badges, plaques, and other objects or commemorative mentions of the personal or collective exaltation of the military uprising, of the Civil War and of the repression of the dictatorship" should be removed from buildings and public spaces."

Again, according to this newspaper article written in October 2014, a budget from Jávea town hall was requested for the purpose of removing the shields. However, it was a large sum of money and at the end of the fiscal year the municipal coffers did not have enough money, hence nothing was done.

It was also pointed out in the article that when the shields should finally be removed that they would not be destroyed but stored in a municipal warehouse, which from a historical point of view made sense.

UPDATE TO ESSAY, Summer 2018

I have read today that 'la Cruz Cubierta de la Plaza del Trinquet" has been given some new hope. The City of Xàbia decided to pay dedication to the master stonemason and architecture of this monument by allowing his name to grace the front corner of it.

Vicente Bisquert Riera, better known as Vicent de Gràcia, left his undoubted artistic footprint as an enterprising person who contributed to the most characteristic works and sculptural elements of Xabia. He created the fountain in the church square, the fountain in the garden square at Loreto Street, the fountain of the Convent square, the balconies of the Abadía (priest's) house, many of the altarpieces, and other sculptural elements of the church-fortress of San Bartolome, in addition to other unique works such as its funerary monument to the old cemetery of Sant Joan.

In honour of Vicente Bisquert Riera, City Council plans to rehabilitate the cross monument because the dome is collapsing and the gargoyles, ashlars, and pilasters will also be repaired. One of the pinnacles will be replaced, among other rehabilitative actions, and the entire monument will be cleaned with water pressure.

It also was proposed that the remaining dictatorship symbols such as the pre-constitutional shield and the yoke and arrows of the Phalanx would be preserved in the Museum thus complying with article 15.1 of Law 52/2007.

NOTE: In the spring of 2020, this monument was altered to comply with the law.

Printed in Great Britain
by Amazon